Rape Hysteria
Lying with Rape Statistics

John Davis, BA., J.D., LL.M.

DEDICATION

This monograph is dedicated to all who work with victims of false accusations of rape, exonerees, prosecutors with integrity, and those who tirelessly defend the innocent.

End Rape *Hysteria*

Prosecute False Accusations

SeXual Assault
Awareness Month

Table of Contents

ACKNOWLEDGMENTS

The Author and Publisher would like to thank Judge Andrew Napolitano and U. S. Magistrate Judge Kristen L. Mix.

RAPE HYSTERIA:
LYING WITH RAPE STATISTICS
By: John Davis, BA., J.D., LL.M.

Lying With Rape Statistics – Rape Statistic Propaganda

Of all the statistics available in the information age, rape statistics are the most elusive.

Statistics on rape are inherently unreliable because of the political, and gynocentric,[1] inter-

---

[1] *Gynocentric*, Syllabification: gy·no·cen·tric ADJECTIVE: Centered on or concerned exclusively with women; taking
a female (or specifically a feminist) point of view. Oxford English Dictionary (2014).

ests that stand to gain from exaggerating the amount of rape that occurs.

Rape is considered such a serious crime, that a mere accusation of rape is sufficient to ruin an accused. Consequently, the power to falsely accuse of rape is a coveted power. It enables someone to invoke massive law enforcement resources, based upon a mere accusation, and, it empowers someone to inflict immense injury on a falsely accused without having to comply with due process. (Even though a majority of rape accusations are proven to be false, the mere accusation, or arrest, of an innocent person on rape charges is sufficient to make that person unemployable, and, a semi-permanent subject of hatred and scorn in any community).

The result is that gynocentric interests ridiculously exaggerate the number of actual rapes that occur.

This exaggeration of the incidence of rape in the U.S. reached hysterical proportions in 2013 and 2014, and, eventually the mainstream media began to question the hysteria.[2]

_____

[2] *See, e.g.,* Will, George, *"Colleges become the victims of progressivism,"* Washington Post (June 6, 2014).
http://www.washingtonpost.com/opinions/george-quewill-college-become-the-victims-of-progressivism/2014/06/06/e90e73b4-eb50-

Once a major mainstream commentator began to apply logic, reason and verifiable statistics to the rape propaganda and hysteria, the mainstream media response was shock, horror and disbelief. Rather than correct the exaggerated statistics, many mainstream media outlets simply engaged in massive denial.

In a typical response, to suppress accurate statistics, and analysis, of the rape hysteria in the U.S. media, many pundits called for the resignation of anyone who questioned that "1 in 5 women on college campuses are raped;" or that " 1 in 4 women will be raped in their lifetime;" or that "rape is an epidemic in our colleges and universities."

These falsified statistics, to make matters worse, usually originated from government sources. Since they originated from government sources, many people mistakenly believed that "they must be true." In truth, the exaggerated statistics are the product of political corruption over those captive agencies.

How is it possible for government statistics to be so corrupted as to represent a fraud on the public?

11e3-9f5c-9075d5508f0a_story.html

To answer this question, one must look at the techniques used by those who profit from the "rape industry" in the U.S. The principal benefactors of rape hysteria are in government itself.

Politicians, by promoting rape hysteria, seek to generate votes for themselves by pretending to be "tough on crime" and "fighting the rape problem in the U.S." These politicians often gain enough votes from rape hysteria to make a difference in an election. Consequently, if one candidate promotes rape hysteria, and, promotes herself as a solution to rape hysteria, then, any other candidate in the election arena must do the same, or risk being labeled "misogynistic."

The second largest pool of benefactors from rape hysteria are the police and law enforcement lobbies. With the war on drugs de-escalating, police agencies need new job and funding justifications. Police agencies therefore promote rape hysteria in order to justify additional funding for their departments and staffing budgets.

The third largest pool of benefactors of rape hysteria are the government agencies, and NGO's, that depend on government funding for their rape programs, and programs related to sexual assault.

The final group which profits from the generated rape hysteria is the world-wide mainstream media. Through shocking headlines, the global mainstream media sells numerous stories and commentaries, each purporting to "expose" a "vast rape epidemic" (much like Senator McCarthy "exposed" purportedly rampant anti-American activities in the 1950's).[3]

U.N. Rape Hysteria Fraud

One example of media hysteria, and rape paranoia involves the United Nations claiming that 1 in 4 Asian men admit to having "raped" their intimate partner. In September of 2013, news outlets around the world, festooned international media feeds with the following headlines:

Almost a quarter of men 'admit to rape in

---

[3] Compare Senator Kirsten Gillibrand's (D-N.Y.) current "sexual assault crusade, with the anti-communist crusade of Senator Joseph McCarthy (R-Wis.) in the 1950's.

parts of Asia[4]

News outlet, after news outlet, spread these headlines across the globe. Not one of the journalists" commenting on this headline made any attempt to analyze the basis for the headline.

The basis for the headline was a United Nations study, done by the U.N. Commission on Women.

On the questionnaire purporting to expose "rape," out of twenty questions, one of the questions was:

"Have you ever had sex with your partner when you knew she didn't want to but you thought she should agree because she's your wife / partner?"

If the man answered this question in the affirmative, he was classified as a rapist. The U.N.'s reasoning for classifying one fourth of the male participants as rapists was that they were rapists not because they forced their partner to

---

[4] Tulip Mazumdar, "Almost a quarter of men 'admit to rape in parts of Asia'," BBC News — Health, September 9, 2013. http://www.bbc.com/news/health-24021573

have sex, but, because they "felt entitled" to sex with their partner even though she might not have wanted to have sex at the time.

There was no control survey done on women to determine how many women would answer the question in the affirmative. However, other studies strongly suggest that women also feel entitled to have sex with their husband or male partner, in a long-term relationship, even if their male partner is not fully "in the mood."[5]

Most rational people who have experienced healthy interpersonal relationships have, at one time or another, in those relationships, had sex with their partner even if they did not want to have sex. This is a normal part of compassionately addressing needs of a partner in an intimate relationship. It is not "rape" except to those who are striving for excuses to raise rape hysteria and paranoia.[6]

---

[5] Charlotte Alter, *"Nearly Half of Young Men Say They Have Had Unwanted Sex,"* Time Magazine, March 25, 2014. http://time.com/37337/nearly-half-of-young-men-say-theyve-had-unwanted-sex/; French, B. H., Tilghman, J. D., & Malebranche, D. A. (2014, March 17). Sexual CoercionContext and Psychosocial Correlates Among Diverse Males. Psychology of Men &Masculinity. Advance online publication. http://dx.doi.org/10.1037/a0035915.

[6] *See,* Ruth Alexander, "How Many Men in Asia Admit to Rape?" BBC

College Campus Rape Hysteria

As another example, in January of 2014, the White House undertook a one-sided campaign to protect women on college campuses from rape and sexual assault.[7] (The campaign openly placed all responsibility for sexual assault on men, and, men alone. The campaign made no effort to address the rate of sexual assault of men on campuses, which is higher than it is for women).

Note: A recent (2002) study commissioned by the National Institute of Mental Health, and conducted by the University of Illinois details

---

News Magazine, November 1, 2013.
http://www.bbc.com/news/magazine-24713110

[7] Jackie Calms, "Obama Seeks to Raise Awareness of Rape on Campus," NEW YORK TIMES, January 22, 2014.
http://www.nytimes.com/2014/01/23/us/politics/obama-to-create-task-force-on-campus-sexual-assaults.html?_r=0

the dynamics of women who rape men.[8]

> Only recently have researchers be-
> gun to examine sexual coercion di-
> rected toward men [citations omit-
> ted] Struckman-Johnson (1988)[9]
> and Struckman-Johnson (1998)[10]
> found 43% of men sampled report-
> ed experiencing a coercive incident,
> of which 36% reported unwanted
> touch and 27% reported being co-
> erced into sexual intercourse. Re-
> search examining both men and
> women as perpetrators and victims
> of coercive or aggressive behavior
> found that men and women experi-
> ence comparable levels of physical
> violence in dating relationships
> (McConaghy & Zamir, 1995;[11] Si-

[8] Debra L. Oswald, PhD, Brenda L. Russell, "Sexual Coercion and Victimization of College Men," 17 J. INTERPERSONAL VIOLENCE 3, pp. 273-285 (March 2002). (One hundred and seventy-three men were recruited from undergraduate courses at a private Midwestern University. Mean age of respondents was 20.94 (SD = 3.48). (n=173).

[9] Struckman-Johnson, C., "Forced sex on dates: It happens to men too." 24 JOURNAL OF SEX RESEARCH 234-241 (1988).

[10] Struckman-Johnson, C., & Struckman-Johnson, D. "The dynamics and impact of sexual coercion of men by women." In P. B. Anderson, & C. Struckman-Johnson (Eds.), "Sexually aggressive women: Current perspectives and controversies" (pp. 121-143). New York: Guilford.

[11] McConaghy, N., & Zamir, R., "Heterosexual and homosexual coercion, sexual orientation and sexual roles in medical students." 24

gelman, Berry, & Wiles, 1984)[12]. . . .
. These studies reveal that victimi-
zation of men occurs with some
regularity; . . . .[13]

These studies show that 27% of college men have been raped by women. (I.e., according to the new federal definitions of rape, the men have been subjected to coerced intercourse without their consent).[14]

In April of 2014, the White House Task Force purportedly assigned to preventing campus sexual assault, issued its first report.[15]

The White House made no effort to conceal its gynocentric, gender-specific campaign. Mainstream media bombarded the public with a

---

ARCHIVES OF SEXUAL BEHAVIOR, 489-502 (1995).

[12] Sigelman, C. K., Berry, C. J., & Wiles, K. A. "Violence in college students' dating relationships," 5 JOURNAL OF APPLIED SOCIAL PSYCHOLOGY, 530-548 (1984).

[13] Oswald & Russell, *supra* at 274.

[14] United States Department of Justice, *An Updated Definition of Rape*, http://blogs.justice.gov/main/archives/1801 January 6, 2012.

[15] "FACT SHEET: Not Alone – Protecting Students from Sexual Assault," White House Office of the Press Secretary, April 14, 2014 http://www.whitehouse.gov/the-press-office/2014/04/29/fact-sheet-not-alone-protecting-students-sexual-assault

fraudulent statistic that claimed 1 in 5 women would be sexually assaulted on college campuses in the U.S.

The White House "statistics," however, were literally a fantasy statistic. The statistic of 1 in 5 women in college being subjected to sexual assault was based entirely on what is known as "advocacy research."[16] ("Advocacy research" is "research" that is not really "research;" it is merely the product of persons who, without any objectivity or any adherence to the scientific method, searches for specious and spurious bits of data, often abstracted out of context, to support their own personal biases and prejudices.)[17]

To make matters worse, careless, or outright deceptive, advocacy journalism began confusing "sexual assault" with "forcible rape." With the typical accuracy of zealots, the mainstream media began disseminating headlines that stated: 1 in 5 women on college campuses will be raped while attending colleges and universities in the

---

[16] Christina Hoff Sommers, "CDC study on sexual violence in the U.S overstates the problem," WASHINGTON POST, January 27, 2012. http://www.washingtonpost.com/opinions/cdc-study-on-sexual-violence-in-the-us-overstates-the-problem/2012/01/25/gIQAHRKPWQ_story.html

[17] Id.

U.S.

The fact is, that according to FBI statistics, in all of the College Campuses and Universities in the U.S., combined, there were only 485 forcible rapes known in a typical college year.

Figure 1 - Popular Facebook Meme 2014

The Effects of Rape Hysteria?

The effects of Rape Hysteria are almost never addressed by either the media or government agencies.

The first effect is that innocent men are frequently arrested on false rape charges.

False accusations of rape would fairly full a complete volume to properly explore. We can only summarize, in this report, the devastating effects on a man who is falsely accused of rape.

There are examples of falsely accused men who have been subjected to severe violence, permanent loss of employment, shunning in the community, and, more devastatingly, false imprisonment or death at the hands of lynch mobs.

We have only to look to our recent, barbaric past in the U.S., and in other countries, to know that men who are falsely accused often lose their lives (without any possibility of due process of law).

Figure 2 - Lynchings of Men falsely accused of rape were common under Jim Crow in the U.S. Many lynchings were conducted based on false accusations prompted by rape hysteria.

Gynocentric political interests are quick to cite a fantasy statistic that only 2% of rape claims are false. However, the 2% figure has been proven to be a sham statistic that has no basis in reality. The 2% figure was a completely contrived figure invented by a novelist in the 1970's. As with most propaganda, it was re-peated endlessly (and erroneously) until it be-came accepted as truth. That figure, of only 2% of rape claims being false, however, has been thoroughly debunked by legal scholars.[18]

The next most common statistic on false rape claims, advanced by gynocentric interests, is a figure that only 8% of rape complaints are false. This figure was taken from stock language in FBI reports that has appeared, for years, in those reports, without any statistical substantiation by the FBI.[19]

The FBI reports, however, if they are carefully read by a person trained as a prosecutor,

---

[18] Edward Greer, The Truth behind Legal Dominance Feminism's Two Percent False Rape Claim Figure, 33 Loy. L.A. L. Rev. 947 (2000). Available at: http://digitalcommons.lmu.edu/llr/vol33/iss3/3

[19] "Complaints of all Crime Index offenses made to law enforcement agencies which are found to be false or baseless can be "unfounded" and excluded from crime counts. A higher percentage of complaints of forcible rape are determined "unfounded," or found by investigation to be false, than for any other Index crime. While the average of "unfounded" rates for all Crime Index offenses was 2 percent in 1997, 8 percent of forcible rape complaints were "unfounded" for the same timeframe." FBI, Uniform Crime Reports for the United states 1997, p. 26. "Nationally, over half of the forcible rapes reported to law enforcement were cleared by arrest or exceptional means during 1997. At 55 percent for suburban counties and 52 percent for rural counties, county law enforcement clearance rates were slightly higher than the city law enforcement clearance rate at 50 percent. (See Table 25.)" Id. In other words, although 8% of rape accusations were definitively determined to be false beyond any doubt, approximately 50% of the remaining accusations of rape had no evidence on which to make an arrest.

show not that the rate of false claims of rape is limited to 8%. The FBI reports show that the incidence of false claims of rape are *at least* 8%. Gynocentric pundits jump to the conclusion that this means that *only* 8% of rape complaints are false.

What inexpert analysts overlook in, jumping to this conclusion, is that just because law enforcement has determined that 8% of rape complaints are definitely false, does not mean that the remaining 92% of rape complaints are true.

In examining the FBI reports, on which people rely for the claim that the rate of false accusations of rape is only 8%, amateur analysts overlook the fact that those same reports state that [only] fifty percent of the rape complaints are "cleared by arrest." What this means, in law enforcement parlance, is that there was insufficient evidence to arrest anyone in 50% of the cases.[20]

---

[20] *See generally*, James McNamara and Jennifer Lawrence, "False Allegations of Adult Crimes," FBI Law Enforcement Bulletin, September 2012. (There are a large number of alleged sex crimes that although do not fall into the category of having been determined as "false," nevertheless fall into the category of being unsupported, or, too speculative as to be considered legitimate claims to form a basis for arrest and prosecution).

As any experienced prosecutor knows, the threshold of evidence required to make an arrest is extremely low. The 1980's and 1990's was a time in which courts dramatically adopted "law and order" rhetoric to remove constitutional protections for due process of law, and, make it almost impossible for a judge to rule that an arrest was made without probable cause. In most cases, the U.S. Supreme Court has lowered the evidentiary threshold for an arrest to the point where there is no effective threshold. The police may arrest someone merely upon an accusation of a complainant, a mere suspicion, or, even upon an anonymous insinuation.[21]

If the police do not have sufficient evidence to make an arrest in 50% of rape cases, although the police may not have definitively determined that those 50% of rape claims are false, it is reasonable to conclude that those 50% of rape claims, for which there is insufficient evidence to make an arrest, are also false claims.

Independent, mainstream studies, confirm this analysis of FBI statistics and reports on false allegations of rape.

---

[21] This is known as a "post-constitutional society." *See generally,* J. Andrew P. Napolitano, "Constitutional Chaos: What Happens When the Government Breaks Its Own Laws," 2006.

The two most cited studies are also those that gynocentric interests most seek to suppress and conceal from the mainstream media.

A look at these sources, however, shows that the studies (although subjected to a barrage of negative rhetoric from feminist groups and those promoting rape hysteria) are sound. They are the only studies that were conducted according to scientific principles, and, remain un-refuted by any other similar studies.

The first study is known as the "*Kanin Study.*"[22]

The *Kanin Study* was conducted before "rape shield" statutes[23] effectively prohibited scientific

---

[22] Eugne Kanin, Ph.D., *False Rape Allegations*, ARCHIVES OF SEXUAL BEHAVIOR, VoL 23, No. L (1994).
http://blog.lib.umn.edu/jbs/maysession/KaninFalseRapeAllegations.pdf

[23] A thorough discussion of "rape shield statutes," and how they impair scientific studies on the subject of false accusations of rape, is beyond the scope of this report. Briefly, rape shield statutes prohibit law enforcement, prosecutors and defense counsel from inquiring into the circumstances of a rape accusation, and details about the rape accuser. Rape shield statutes, effectively, require that law enforcement or prosecutors, and courts, minimize the efforts to question the validity of a rape claimant's allegations as to whether or not the allegation is true. There is little dispute among law enforcement personnel that rape shield statutes are responsible for many false accusations of rape, and, impair the integrity of investigations into claims of rape that are well-founded, as well as those that are spurious or false.

and objective inquiries into actual rape cases.

The *Kanin Study* is actually in two parts. Dr. Kanin first analyzed rape cases at a Midwestern city's police department. About 41% of the women who had made complaints that they had been raped, on further investigation, admitted that their rape complaints were false. There was a sufficient number of participants to allow Kanin to infer that, in the general population of rape complaints, about 41% of rape claims are false (with a margin of error of about 7 points).

However, several years after the first study, Kanin duplicated the experiment using campus police in Indianapolis (at Purdue University). The second study affirmed the first, and, showed that roughly 60% of rape complaints made to law enforcement were also false.

Dr. Kanin eventually concluded, through expert analysis, in a large population, nationwide, a report of rape was as likely to be false as it was to be true.

The second study, often suppressed as being "politically incorrect," and often assaulted by gynocentric interests, is a U. S. Air Force Study conducted by the U. S. Air Force Office of Special Investigations in 1984.[24] This study also pre-dates rape shield statutes and stands as one of the few scientifically based studies on the real rate of false accusations of rape. Like the *Kanin* study, gynocentric interests have viciously assaulted the study with rhetoric, and censored it, but there are no credible studies that contradict it.

This report, which was also based upon the unimpeachable admissions of the women making rape complaints that the allegations were false, fix the rate of false allegations of rape at about 65%.

A more recent report in the Forensic Examiner, by Dr. Bruce Gross, Ph.D., J.D., M.B.A., also confirms the actual rate of false accusations is somewhere between 50% and 60%.[25] Dr. Gross, in his paper, provides an extensive analysis of the phenomenon of false rape accu-

---

[24] "False Allegations," FORENSIC SCIENCE DIGEST, V. 11, no. 4, Dec. 1985, p. 64, by Charles P. McDowell. The websites containing Col. McDowell's Air Force report are often "hacked" to keep people from accessing the report online. However, with some diligence, copies of the report may be found in various locations on the internet.

[25] Bruce Gross, Ph.D., J.D., M.B.A, False Rape Allegations – An Assault on Justice, 2 FORENSIC EXAMINER (Spring 2009). http://www.theforensicexaminer.com/archive/spring09/15/

sations in our current climate of rape hysteria in the U.S. (and abroad).

What is the real rate of rape in the U.S.?

Our research for this work indicates that there are some reliable statistics available on the real incidence of rape. However, there are almost no reliable *analyses* of those rape statistics available.

The FBI has published an often suppressed statistic on the incidence of rape in the U.S. The FBI's statistic is that the incidence of rape is 26.9 rapes per 100,000 people in the U.S. Based upon a population estimate of 313,914,040 people in the United States, there were, in 2012, approximately 84,443 forcible rapes **reported** in the U.S. general population.

Although this is a "hard statistic," and would seem to indicate that there were 84,443 forcible rapes in the U.S. in 2012, it is important to realize that not all "reported rapes" constitute actual incidents of rape.[26]

In determining the actual rate of rape, in the U.S., one must take some factors into consideration and adjust the statistics.

The first factor is the amount of false rape reports. Our research conclusively established that roughly 60% of "reported rapes" are false. (See discussion, *supra,* and notes accompanying).

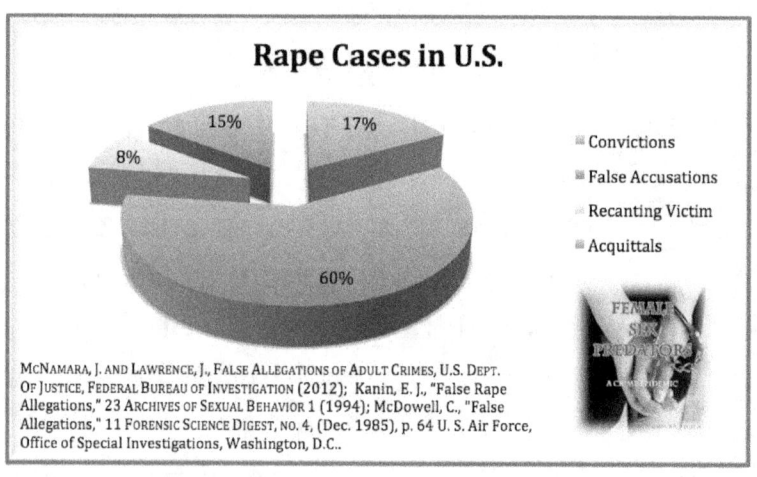

Rape Cases in U.S.

- Convictions
- False Accusations
- Recanting Victim
- Acquittals

17% 15% 8% 60%

McNamara, J. and Lawrence, J., False Allegations of Adult Crimes, U.S. Dept. of Justice, Federal Bureau of Investigation (2012); Kanin, E. J., "False Rape Allegations," 23 Archives of Sexual Behavior 1 (1994); McDowell, C., "False Allegations," 11 Forensic Science Digest, No. 4, (Dec. 1985), p. 64 U. S. Air Force, Office of Special Investigations, Washington, D.C..

---

[26] *See generally,* James McNamara and Jennifer Lawrence, *False Allegations of Adult Crimes,* FBI Law Enforcement Bulletin, September 2012. (There are a large number of alleged sex crimes that although do not fall into the category of having been determined as "false," nevertheless fall into the category of being unsupported, or, too speculative as to be considered legitimate claims to form a basis for arrest and prosecution).

Figure 3 - Concise statistical representation of disposition of rape cases reported to law enforcement in the U.S. (based mostly on FBI crime reports)

About half of the rapes that are taken to trial result in acquittals, and another 8% of "reported rapes" result in exonerations (with the accuser recanting the accusation of rape, or DNA evidence exonerating the accused).

The chart above shows the statistical adjustments that must be made to the number of "reported rapes" in order to arrive at an accurate number of actual forcible rapes.

Realistically, only 17% of "reported rape" cases are actual cases of rape. This would seem to indicate that the actual number of rapes occurring in the U.S. in 2012 was 14,355 rapes. That figure yields an adjusted statistical probability of a woman being raped, in a given year, at one in 11,371. (We would emphasize that even one case of forcible rape is abhorrent in any culture. However, we would also emphasize that the rate at which men are raped by women, likely exceeds the rate at which men rape women. Consequently, we believe that statistics must begin to reflect the actual rate of rape that includes the incidents of women who rape men.

This is the subject of another of our studies).[27]

However, to arrive at an accurate figure of rape, one must make another major adjustment.

The FBI statistics do NOT include the numbers of women who rape men in which men are the victims and women are the offenders. The numbers of women who rape men have been intentionally excluded from federal statistics up until January of 2012.

With the U.S. Department of Justice finally providing a gender neutral definition of rape, we may see accurate statistics, and, accurate analysis of those statistics in the near future.

However, for now, it is clear that the real incidence of rape in the U.S., and globally, is only a small fraction of the rate of rape that is promoted by government offices and the mainstream media.

A Case Study of Media Rape Hysteria

---

[27] Davis, John, BA., J.D., Ll.M., "Women Who Rape Men," 2014. (Available on Amazon Kindle Books).

On May 27, 2014, tragically, two girls about age 14 were found hanging by their necks in a tree in Badaun, India.

Within hours, the international media began a crisis escalation by reporting that the girls had been "gang raped," and, that this was a part of an extensive pattern of sexual violence against women in India, and the rest of the world.

Figure 4 – Falsified photograph, distributed world-wide by mainstream media outlets. The photograph was "photoshopped" by feminist organizations in India and distributed to the global mainstream media to raise hysteria regarding sexual crimes against women in India.

The headlines, accompanied by (falsified photos) declared:

"**Teen girls gang-raped and hanged from a tree – police.**"[28] (In fact, the police had never suspected that the girls had been raped, nor did they ever report to anyone that the girls had been raped).

"**Outrage over gang rape, murder of cousins in U.P. village**"[29] (In fact, Western news media paid a few hundred people to assemble to make it appear that there was mass concern over the (unfortunate) death of the girls and the purported rape.

"**Badaun Gang Rape: Two of the Accused Confess to Crime**"[30] (In fact, five men were accused by the parents of the girls of rape, and were jailed, but none of them ever confessed. Eventually, after months

---

[28] Bhalla, Nita (29 May 2014). "Teen girls gang-raped and hanged from a tree - police". New Delhi: Reuters. Retrieved May 30, 2014.

[29] CK, Chandramohan (30 May 2014). "Outrage over gang rape, murder of cousins in U.P. village". Badaun: The Hindu. Retrieved May 30, 2014

[30] Badaun Gang Rape: Two of the Accused Confess to Crime". *Outlook*. 1 June 2014. Retrieved 1 June 2014.

of thorough investigations, all charges were dropped against the five men).

On June 2, 2014, the United Nations issued a statement condemning the gang-rape saying: "There should be justice for families of the two teenage girls ... Violence against women is a human rights issue, not a women's issue. Violence against women is preventable, not inevitable ... The Badaun incident highlights the dangers women in India are exposed to due to lack of toilets." [31] In a statement, Lise Grande, the UN's resident coordinator for India, said, "There should be justice for the families of the two teenage girls and for all the women and girls from lower-caste communities who are targeted and raped in rural India".[32]

---

[31] Jason Burke, "Indian gang-rape girl's family say they have been threatened with violence," The Guardian, June 3, 2014. http://www.theguardian.com/world/2014/jun/03/india-gang-rape-family-threats

[32] "Indian police use water cannon to end gang-rape protest in Lucknow," The Guardian, June 2, 2014. http://www.theguardian.com/world/2014/jun/02/india-police-gang-rape-protest-lucknow-uttar-pradesh," Times of India, June 4, 2014. http://timesofindia.indiatimes.com/india/UN-chief-Ban-Ki-moon-appalled-by-Badaun-gang-rape-case-demands-action/articleshow/36043470.cms

On June 4, 2014, Ban Ki moon con-
demned the rape case and spoke against
the violence against women that is
spreading across the world. He also con-
demned the destructive attitude of "boys
will be
boys".[33]http://en.wikipedia.org/wiki/2014_Badaun_gang_ra
pe - cite_note-37

What really happened?

What really happened to the two young girls
is still not certain. After months of investigations, lie detector tests, forensic studies, multi-
ple autopsies[34] and police investigations by
more than three different law enforcement agencies, the only thing that is clear is that the girls
died by strangulation but they were never raped

---

[33] UN chief Ban Ki-moon appalled by Badaun gang-rape case, demands
action, Times of India, June 4, 2014.
http://timesofindia.indiatimes.com/india/UN-chief-Ban-Ki-moon-appalled-
by-Badaun-gang-rape-case-demands-action/articleshow/36043470.cms

[34] Badaun Case: CBI Exhumes Bodies of Two Girls," New Delhi Television, July 19, 2014; http://www.ndtv.com/article/india/badaun-case-
cbi-exhumes-bodies-of-two-girls-561411

or sexually assaulted.[35]

It is possible that the two girls committed suicide.

Because of the hysteria that immediately arose in the international media, five men were arrested and detained for months based on false accusations of the parents. The five men eventually exonerated themselves by all five of them passing lie-detector tests, [36] and, because there was virtually no evidence against them other than accusations by the girls' parents.

In addition, with regard to the accusations of the girls' parents, none of the parents or accusers passed a lie detector test – they all failed. Police suspect the parent accusers, themselves, of having murdered the girls.[37]

---

[35] Aditya Kalra, "Forensic Report Complicates India Double Rape Murder Case," Reuters Wire, August 22, 2014 "(Reuters) - Indian federal investigators are analyzing a forensic report that found that two teenage girls, earlier believed to have been raped before they were murdered, were not sexually assaulted."

[36] Sunetra Choudhury, "Badaun Gang-Rape Case: Five Accused Pass Lie Detector Tests, Say Sources" New Delhi Television, August 06, 2014 18:03 IST; http://www.ndtv.com/article/india/badaun-gang-rape-case-five-accused-pass-lie-detector-tests-say-sources-571732

[37] "Main witness in Badaun gang-rape case fails lie-detector test:

What is also clear is that this terrible tragedy had nothing to do with rape, gang-rape, men in general, or any "rape culture" that routinely promotes violence against women.

The "gang rape" which received instant world-wide media distribution was nothing more than poor journalism, fraud and hysteria. Most of the fraudulent media stories were disseminated to Western journalists by gynocentric political and media interests who sought to gain political influence, government budget increases and gynosympathy from the falsified rape incident.

India is not a country in which women are at great risk for rape. Nor is it a country in which men are pre-disposed to rape women. Rather, it is a country that exploits rape hysteria to perpetuate a system in which women are privileged, and, in which that privilege accelerates because of the rape hysteria.

Fully, 53% of accusations of rape in India are false, and that figure is conservative based upon

---

CBI," Times of India, September 18, 2014.
http://timesofindia.indiatimes.com/india/Main-witness-in-Badaun-gang-rape-case-fails-lie-detector-test-CBI/articleshow/42731203.cms

estimates from Indian feminist groups.[38] Some districts of India have a false rate of rape accusations that exceed 93%.

One of the causes of this rape hysteria, and its vile system of false accusations of rape, lies in the system of Indian government which rewards women for making false accusations of rape. At this time, if any crime occurs whatsoever in which the victim is a woman, it is likely that the woman will accuse someone of rape just so that she can obtain a reward ("victim compensation") from the Indian government of up to $200,000.00.[39] The reward is payable almost immediately upon a woman making an accusation of rape whether the accusation is true or false.

It is likely that this "rape hysteria" is spreading to Western countries. For example, the government paid a woman in California, Wanetta

_____

[38] "53% rape cases filed between April 2013 and July 2013 false: Delhi Commission of Women." DNA, October 14, 2014; http://www.dnaindia.com/india/report-53-rape-cases-filed-between-april-2013-and-july-2013-false-delhi-commission-of-women-2023334

[39] "Rape Victims in India to Get up to Rs 2 lakh victim compensation," Infochange (Women), http://infochangeindia.org/women/news/rape-victims-in-india-to-get-rs-2-lakh-compensation.html

Gibson, for falsely accusing an N.F.L. football player, Brian Banks, of rape. She was eventually caught on video tape confessing that her accusation was false, but, not before Mr. Banks had spent four years in prison for a crime he did not commit.[40]

In conclusion, it is clear, that rape hysteria threatens the integrity of our legal system, and the freedom of individuals to an extent not seen in Western culture from any other form of hysteria in Western history.

Cultural Effects of Misandry and Rape Hysteria

There are a number of pronounced effects on our culture, and justice system, which arise from this hysteria.

This first effect is a widespread misandry (hatred of men), that arises from a populace that

---

[40] "Brian Banks' accuser caught on video confessing that Rape Accusation Was Fake," Huffington Post, June 8, 2012. http://www.huffingtonpost.com/2012/06/08/brian-banks-accuser-caugh_n_1581605.html

has been brainwashed into believing that "all men are rapists," and, that rape is so common that it is guaranteed that men will rape women whenever the opportunity arises.

Figure 5 - Popular Facebook meme 2014

These pernicious stereotypes saturate modern media, government "studies," films, television shows, news programs and virtually every form of mass media in the U.S. and around the world.

The cultural result is that many women live in constant terror and fear of being raped. Mass media, politicians and various industries prey upon this fear, that women have about men, and create a *circulus vitiosis* (vicious circle). Women are naturally, and understandably afraid of being raped by men. The media (with the support of many fraudulent studies) not on-ly validates this fear, but persuades women that their fear must become the most important view of their relationships in our culture.

Preying upon women's fears of being raped, mainstream media, for profit, seizes on every opportunity to report every possible salacious accusation against men. It makes no difference if the accusations are true or false. The main-stream media reaps fortunes in revenues simply by distributing the accusations in headlines, news programs, talk shows and even, in exag-gerated form, in fictional TV dramas and film. "Sex sells," and the mainstream corporate media has learned that rape hysteria is a profitable media enterprise.

Men and women, being constantly bombard-ed with the sensationalism of false, or dubious

accusations of rape, have come to believe in recent decades that "rape culture" is prevalent in
the U.S. (and other parts of the world). This
hysteria necessarily implies that strict laws are
necessary, against men (but not against wom-
en), based upon the myths that "all men are
rapists" and "only women can be raped."

This pointed sexism, demonizing all men, is
the fundamental basis for a culture of misandry
(hatred of men) that is common in the U.S. and
other Western cultures. Because many men
still perceive their daughters and wives as their
own property, men can be some of the worst
misandrists when it comes to demonizing other
men, and accelerating the misandry that is an
effect of rape hysteria. Men who view their
daughters and wives as their own property are
typically ferocious supporters of rape hysteria,
misandry, and violence against other men based
solely upon accusations of rape, irrespective of
whether there is any proof of rape.

The Roots of Rape Hysteria – "The Psychic Mech-
anism of Hysterical Phenomena"

Dr. Sigmund Freud identified the source of rape hysteria in the later part of the nineteenth century.

In his 1920 papers "Three Contributions to the Theory of Sex" Dr. Freud examined the concepts of hysteria related to sexual impulses. His theories are complex, but, are subject to simplified explanations (even if feminist theorists abhor those medical explanations). It is important to read his 1920 papers in conjunction with his monograph: "Studies on Hysteria: Nervous and Mental Disease Monograph Series, No. 4."

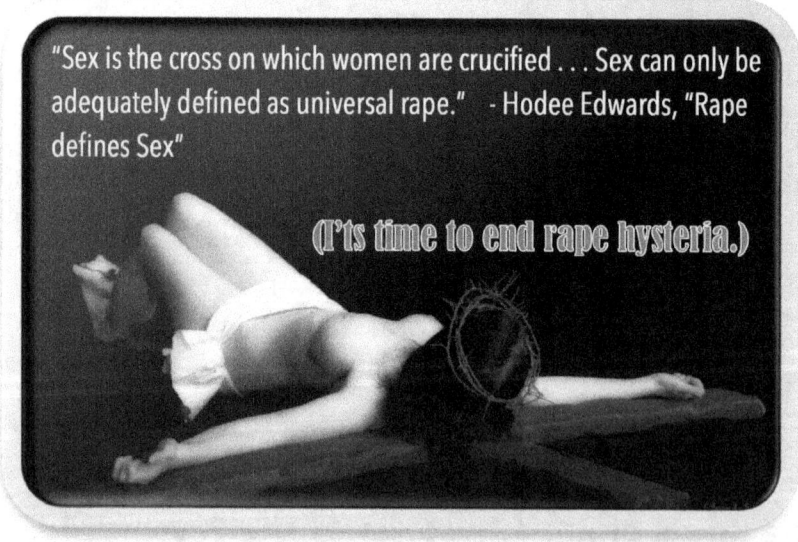

"Sex is the cross on which women are crucified . . . Sex can only be adequately defined as universal rape."   - Hodee Edwards, "Rape defines Sex"

(I'ts time to end rape hysteria.)

Freud has given science a clear explanation of how women's desires for sex, and rape fantasies, frequently cause them to act out serious neuroses, neurotic behavior, and to become hysterical in their response to even consensual normal sex. Many of Freud's cases noted that that hysterical women frequently "remembered" being raped (usually by a family member).

Freud pointed out, in his mature observations [*Verführungstheorie*], that most of these "memories" were false, and, were simply the product of women's latent desires to be raped by men, (rape fantasies), especially their father.

Freud labeled this "The *Oedipus* Complex" (and later developed a special complex for women, similar to the *Oedipus* Complex, known as "The *Electra* Complex.")

[The *Oedipus* Complex derives from the ancient work of Sophocles known as "*Oedipus Rex*" [Oedipus the King] [Οἰδίπους Τύραννος]. In the tragedy, Oedipus Rex, Oedipus kills his Father, and, unknowingly marries his mother and makes her his queen. Freud found that many young boys compete with their Father for their mother's affections, and, wish to rid the family of their father so that they can take his place with their mother. The *Electra* Complex is similar, and also comes from a tragedy written by Sophocles: λέκτρα, except that in the Electra Complex, Freud found most young girls compete with their mother for their Father's affection, and, wish to engage in intimate relationship with their Father].

In "The *Electra* Complex" Freud describes how women (as children) have intense desires for sex with their Father. They are taught to repress these intense feelings. The repression of these feelings produce hysteria in the adult women, which cause them to, in many cases, report that they have been raped or molested by their Father, (or other men), when in fact they have often not even had any intimate contact with the male object of their repressed sexual desires. Freud explains the psychodynamics of this form of false rape accusation hysteria as follows:

The hysterical character evinces a part of sexual repression which reaches beyond the normal limits, an exaggeration of the resistances against the sexual impulse, which we know as shame and loathing. It is an instinctive flight from intellectual occupation with the sexual problem, the consequence of which in pronounced cases is a complete sexual ignorance, which is preserved till the age of sexual maturity is attained."[41]

In other words, women frequently regret having sex with a man, and their regret (shame and loathing) causes them to falsely accuse the man of rape (or some form of non-consensual sexual activity) sometimes in later years.

Freud's brilliant analysis, formed from hundreds of first-hand case studies, explains the high rate of false accusations in Western culture.

It is important to note that modern feminists vociferously denounce Freud with everything from *ad hominem* attacks to personal insults and ridicule.

The Feminist attacks on Freud's theories, however, are without substance or any scientific basis. Contemporary researchers have validated Freud's "theories" with meticulous scientific studies.[42]

---

[41] Freud, Sigmund, "Three Contributions to the Theory of Sex," (The Sexual Aberrations), Vienna 1920. Studien über Hysterie, 1895, J. Breuer tells of a patient on whom he first practiced the cathartic method: "The sexual factor was surprisingly undeveloped."

[42] Selma Aybek, MD; Timothy R. Nicholson, MD, Ph.D.; Fernando Zelaya, PhD; Owen G. O'Daly, PhD; Tom J. Craig, MD, PhD; Anthony S. David, MD; Richard A. Kanaan, MD, PhD, "Neural Corre-

There are additional contemporary studies which validate Freud's theories well beyond the shallow criticisms of modern feminism. In her doctoral thesis in 2008, Dr. Jenny M. Bivona published the results of her research on "Women's Erotic Rape Fantasies."

Dr. Bivona notes in her thesis that the incidence of rape fantasies among women are common, with 55-60% of women reporting having a rape fantasy at least once per month, and the median experience of rape fantasies occurring in those women three times each month.[43]

Perhaps not coincidentally, the rate of false accusations of rape in the U.S. are about the same at 55% - 60%.

---

lates of Recall of Life Events in Conversion Disorder," 71 JAMA Psychiatry 1 (January 2014); *See e.g.* Gale, Jason, "Freud's Hysteria Theory Backed by Patients' Brain Scans," Bloomberg (Businessweek), February 17, 2014.

[43] Shulman, J. L., & Horne, S. G. (2006). Guilty or not? A path model of women's forceful sexual fantasies. Manuscript submitted for publication.

Conclusions

Rape is a serious crime, with serious consequences for both male and female victims. However, fortunately, rape is relatively rare.

Unfortunately, government sources and mainstream media sources, on the subject of the incidence of rape are not reliable. Those sources are, more often than not, politically skewed and, at times, fraudulent to serve special interests.

It is imperative that those persons interested in the real rate of forcible rape, in the U.S. and across the world, seriously question any reported information in mainstream media sources, government sources, and advocacy "research sources" before relying upon either statistics or common impressions on the subject of rape and sexual assault.

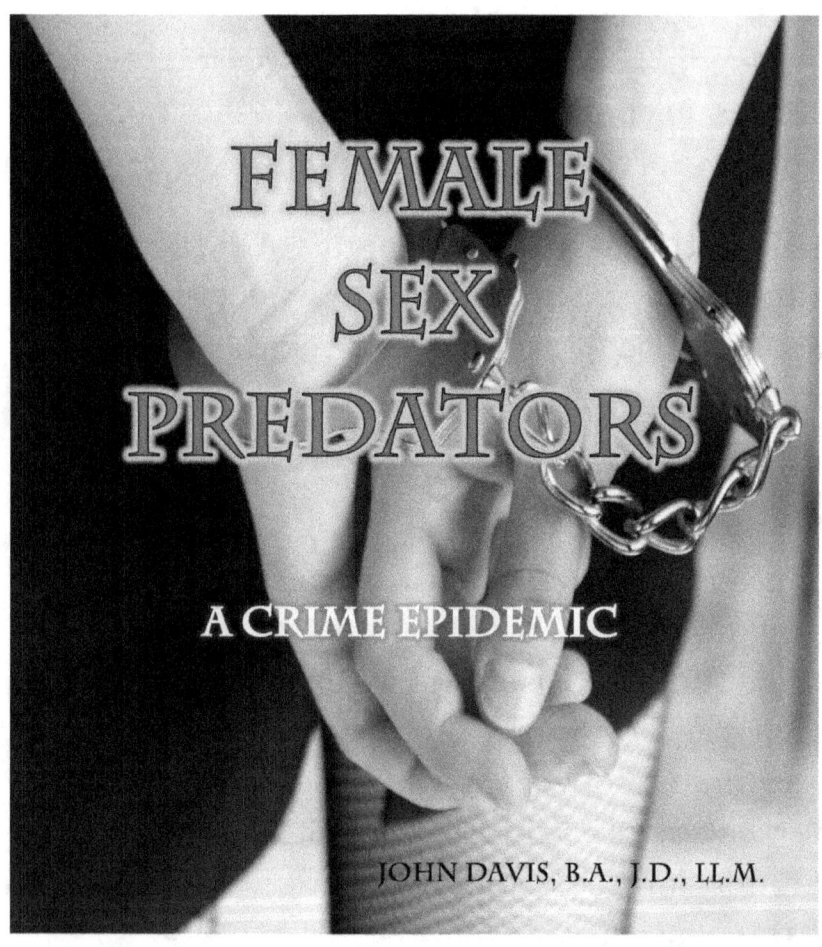

ABOUT THE AUTHOR

John Davis (1953 -) was born in Cleveland, Ohio. He was educated at Case Western Reserve University (BA) (one of the top ten universities in the United States), Seattle University School of Law (JD), and, New York University School of Law (LL.M post-doctoral) (one of the top ten law schools in the United States). John is fluent in seven languages (including ancient Latin and Greek). He has travelled the world over, many times, and has represented clients, in his thirty five year career, such as the United States Government and the Federation of Russia.

He has been a prosecutor three times in his 35 year career. He has held positions such as Assistant Attorney General (State of Arizona), United States Speaker, and Deputy District Attorney.

For most of his career in civil law, John was a successful international lawyer, practicing in many nations around the world.

John is now retired and lives in the South of France.